Auroville Form Style and Design

towards new forms for a new consciousness

Text by Sri Aurobindo
The National Value of Art
and other texts by The Mother

Copyright: Prisma, Auroville
Author: Franz Fassbender
Photographs: John Mandeen

Second edition: 2015

ISBN: 978-93-95460-16-3 (Paperpack)
ISBN: 978-93-95460-17-0 (ebook)

BISAC Code:
ARC005000, ARCHITECTURE / History / General
ARC007000, ARCHITECTURE / Interior Design / General
ARC015000, ARCHITECTURE / Professional Practice
ARC012000, ARCHITECTURE / Reference
ARC020000, ARCHITECTURE / Regional
ARC013000, ARCHITECTURE / Study & Teaching
ARC025000, ARCHITECTURE / Vernacular
HOM003000, HOUSE & HOME / Decorating & Furnishings
HOM004000, HOUSE & HOME / Design & Construction

Thema Subject Category:
AMA, Theory of architecture
AMR, Architecture: interior design
AMX, History of architecture
AMV, Landscape architecture and design
AMCR, Environmentally-friendly ('green') architecture and design
AMD, Architecture: professional practice
WJK, Interior design, decor and style guides

Cataloging-in-Publication Data for this title is available from the Library of Congress.

Digital Editions produced by:
DMI Systems Pvt Ltd, Vishnupuri,
Aligarh 202001, Uttar Pradesh, India
www.dmi.systems

Published by:
PRISMA, Aurelec/ Prayogshala, Auroville 605101,
Tamil Nadu, India
www.prisma.haus

ACKNOWLEDGEMENTS

The texts by Sri Aurobindo and the Mother are copyright of the Sri Aurobindo Ashram Trust, Pondicherry, and are reproduced here with acknowledgement and thanks to the Trustees.

A dream

There should be somewhere upon earth a place that no nation could claim as its sole property, a place where all human beings of good will, sincere in their aspiration, could live freely as citizens of the world, obeying one single authority, that of the supreme Truth; a place of peace, concord, harmony, where all the fighting instincts of man would be used exclusively to conquer the causes of his suffering and misery, to surmount his weakness and ignorance, to triumph over his limitations and incapacities; a place where the needs of the spirit and the care for progress would get precedence over the satisfaction of desires and passions, the seeking for pleasures and material enjoyment.

In this place, children would be able to grow and develop integrally without losing contact with their soul. Education would be given, not with a view to passing examinations and getting certificates and posts, but for enriching the existing faculties and bringing forth new ones. In this place, titles and positions would be supplanted by opportunities to serve and organise.

The needs of the body will be provided for equally in the case of each and every one. In the general organisation intellectual, moral and spiritual superiority will find expression not in the enhancement of the pleasures and powers of life but in the increase of duties and responsibilities.

Artistic beauty in all forms, painting, sculpture, music, literature, will be available equally to all, the opportunity to share in the joys they bring being limited solely by each one's capacities and not by one's social or financial position.

For in this ideal place money would be no more the sovereign lord. Individual merit will have a greater importance than the value due to material wealth and social position. Work would not be there as the means of gaining one's livelihood, it would be the means whereby to express oneself, develop one's capacities and possibilities, while doing at the same time service to the whole group, which on its side would provide for each one's subsistence and for the field of his work.

In brief, it would be a place where relations between human beings, usually based almost exclusively upon competition and strife, would be replaced by relations of emulation for doing better, for collaboration, relations of real brotherhood.

The Mother

**The whole organisation... was ready
in the subtle physical**

I saw X today and I was telling that the whole organisation
of the arts and sports, even of food and all the rest, was
ready in the subtle physical – ready to come down and
embody itself – and I told him:

   "What is needed is just a handful of earth *(gesture of
cupping the hands)*, a handful of earth where one could
grow the plant…. One must find a handful of earth to let
it grow."

The Mother

Excavation work for the Matrimandir 1971

The Matrimandir will be the soul of Auroville, and the sooner it is there, the better it will be for everyone, especially for the Aurovilians.

The Mother

The Matrimandir wants to be the symbol of the Divine's answer to man's aspiration for perfection. Union with the Divine manifesting in a progressive human unity.

The Mother

Early casurina, bamboo with keet structures

Casurina, bamboo and keet structures of the community kitchen 1971

In the physical the Divine manifests as Beauty.

To cultivate, intellectualise, refine them...

Usually all education, all culture, all refinement of the senses and the being is one of the best ways of curing instincts, desires, passions. To eliminate these things does not cure them; to cultivate, intellectualise, refine them, this is the surest means of curing.

The Mother

One must learn always

One must learn always not only intellectually but also psychologically, one must progress in regard to character, one must cultivate the qualities and correct the defects; everything should be made an occasion to cure ourselves of ignorance and incapacity; life becomes then tremendously interesting and worth the trouble of living it.

Future art

... quite recently, I suddenly felt this, this sensation of something very new, something of the future pushing, pushing, trying to manifest, trying to express itself and not succeeding, but something which will be a terrific progress over all that has been felt and expressed before...

The Mother

Last School, 1970

Skill is not art

Skill is not art, talent is not art. Art is a living harmony and beauty that must be expressed in all the movements of existence. This manifestation of beauty and harmony is part of the Divine realisation upon earth, perhaps even its greatest part.

The Mother

Inside Last School

The aesthetic is of immense importance

The first and lowest use of art is the purely aesthetic, the second is the intellectual or educative, the third and highest the spiritual. By speaking of the aesthetic use as the lowest, we do not wish to imply that it is not of immense value to humanity, but simply to assign to it its comparative value in relation to the higher uses. The aesthetic is of immense importance, and until it has done its work mankind is not really fitted to make full use of art on the higher planes of human development.

Aristotle was speaking of the purification of feelings, passions and emotions in the heart through imaginative treatment in poetry, but the truth the idea contains is of much wider application and constitutes the justification of the aesthetic side of art. It purifies by beauty. The beautiful and the good are held by many thinkers to be the same and, though the idea may be wrongly stated, it is, when put from the right standpoint, not only a truth but the fundamental truth of existence. According to our

own philosophy the whole world came out of *ānanda* and returns into *ānanda*, and the triple term in which *ānanda* may be stated is Joy, Love, Beauty. To see divine beauty in the whole world, man, life, nature, to love that which we have seen and to have pure unalloyed bliss in that love and that beauty is the appointed road by which mankind as a race must climb to God.

At a certain stage of human development the aesthetic sense is of infinite value in this direction. It raises and purifies conduct by instilling a distaste for the coarse desires and passions of the savage, for the rough, uncouth and excessive in action and manner, and restraining both feeling and action by a striving after the decent, the beautiful, the fit and seemly, which received its highest expression in the manners of cultivated European society, the elaborate ceremonious life of the Confucian, the careful ācāra and etiquette of Hinduism.

Sri Aurobindo

Sanskrit School

But it must be beautiful and delightful

The good must not be subordinated to the aesthetic sense, but it must be beautiful and delightful, or to that extent it ceases to be good. The object of existence is not the practice of virtue for its own sake but *ānanda*, delight, and progress consists not in rejecting beauty and delight, but in rising from the lower to the higher, the less complete to the more complete beauty and delight.

God as beauty, Sri Krishna in Brindavan, Shyama-sundara, is not only Beauty, He is also Love, and without perfect love there cannot be perfect beauty, and without perfect beauty there cannot be perfect delight.

Sri Aurobindo

After School

After School

Why it is important to study

Studies strengthen the mind and turn its concentration away from the impulses and desires of the vital. Concentrating on study is one of the most powerful ways of controlling the mind and the vital; that is why it is so important to study.

The Mother

Last School, 2011

A great step forward in the perfection

The system of education which, instead of keeping artistic training apart as a privilege for a few specialists, frankly introduces it as a part of culture no less necessary than literature or science, will have taken a great step forward in the perfection of national education and the general diffusion of a broad based human culture.

Sri Aurobindo

Last School Amphitheatre, 2011

Residential house

When you feel that you know nothing then you are ready to learn.

The Mother

Language Laboratory

Town Hall

The aspect of beauty

Art is nothing less in its fundamental truth than
the aspect of beauty of the Divine manifestation.

The Mother

West end of Town Hall,
with sculptures by Roger Anger

Matrimandir

Mother's bust

Beauty is his footprint showing us

where he has passed

Sri Aurobindo

Behind a few figures, a few trees and rocks the supreme Intelligence, the supreme Imagination, the supreme Energy lurks, acts, feels, is, and, if the artist has the spiritual vision, he can see it and suggest perfectly the great mysterious Life in its manifestations brooding in action, active in thought, energetic in stillness, creative in repose, full of a mastering intention in that which appears blind and unconscious.

Sri Aurobindo

On beauty

There is a classical Sanskrit phrase *Satyam Shivam Sundaram*. Apparently beauty is a divine attribute. Being a divine attribute, it is appreciated and adored by the whole humankind. The famous poet Keats has said:

A thing of beauty is a joy for ever.

He also says:

Beauty is Truth, Truth Beauty – that is all ye know on earth and all ye need to know.

Truly speaking there are all kinds of beauty. As the Mother has said, *"On the physical plane it's in beauty that the Divine expresses Himself."* She also adds, *"In the physical world, of all things it is beauty that expresses best the Divine. The physical world is the world of form and the perfection of form is beauty."*

Here it will be pertinent to say that on the physical plane architecture is one of the precious instruments for the expression of beauty. We know that the Mother wanted Auroville to be a city of beauty, and she knew that modern architecture is producing monstrous buildings which may be suitable for commerce and industry alone. But with skill, the architect can provide for the needs of everyone with a sense of beauty in the whole structure. And for this purpose she chose an architect, Roger Anger of Paris, who had also a firm sense of beauty for architectural design. That is what he was trying to do in Paris, but got a full scope for his genius in Auroville. All visitors to Auroville can see it, and the Matrimandir is the first example of it.

There is not only the beauty of form. The Mother says, *"Let beauty be your constant ideal.*

The beauty of the soul

The beauty of sentiments

The beauty of thoughts

The beauty of the action

The beauty of the work.

She further says,

Spiritual beauty has a contagious power

*

Beauty is the joyous offering of nature.

Elsewhere, in reply to a letter the Mother says, *"There is behind all things a divine beauty, a divine harmony; it is with this that we must come into contact; it is this that we must express."*

In our country, of course, it is a sad fact that the British system of education, which we have had for so long, has been soul-less and ignores our roots and culture. This has gone into decreasing our sense of appreciation of beauty that we had in the past, and which we must now resuscitate, if we are to go ahead with our aim of renaissance and resurgence.

If we regain our sense of beauty, the value of our life will certainly increase. As Sri Aurobindo has said, "A nation surrounded daily by the beautiful, noble, fine and harmonious becomes that which it is habituated to contemplate and realises the fullness of the expanding Spirit in itself." Thus Sri Aurobindo made the point that we all should develop our aesthetic faculty and we should be habituated to accept the beautiful in preference to the ugly.

On the surface, it may not sound so, but in reality it is a truth that for the achievement of the goal of India's renaissance and resurgence, we should make efforts in all sincerity to revive our innate sense of beauty and restore our old glory. Not only the old glory, we can carry it a step further by the descent of the new consciousness and force brought down by Sri Aurobindo and the Mother and which is at work.

Let us aspire for a glorified body of beauty. For we now end with what we started with in the beginning, that is:

Satyam Shivam Sundaram
and
Beauty is Truth, Truth Beauty – that is all ye know on earth and all ye need to know.

Sri Aurobindo's Action

Kala Kendra

Bharat Nivas

The spirit needs all the possible help of the material body

Architecture, sculpture and painting, because they are the three great arts which appeal to the spirit through the eye, are those too in which the sensible and the invisible meet with the strongest emphasis on themselves and yet the greatest necessity of each other. The form with its insistent masses, proportions, lines, colours, can here only justify them by their service for the something intangible it has to express; the spirit needs all the possible help of the material body to interpret itself to itself through the eye, yet asks of it that it shall be as transparent a veil as possible of its own greater significance.

Sri Aurobindo

Bronze sculpture by Robert Lorrain

Peace Table at the Unity Pavilion

If the eye is trained

The mind is profoundly influenced by what it sees and, if the eye is trained from the days of childhood to the contemplation and understanding of beauty, harmony and just arrangement in line and colour, the tastes, habits and character will be insensibly trained to follow a similar law of beauty, harmony and just arrangement in the life of the adult man. This was the great importance of the universal proficiency in the arts and crafts or the appreciation of them which was prevalent in ancient Greece, in certain European ages, in Japan and in the better days of our own history.

Sri Aurobindo

Peace Table, a symbol of peace, George Nakashima

Beauty

In the physical the Divine manifests as Beauty.

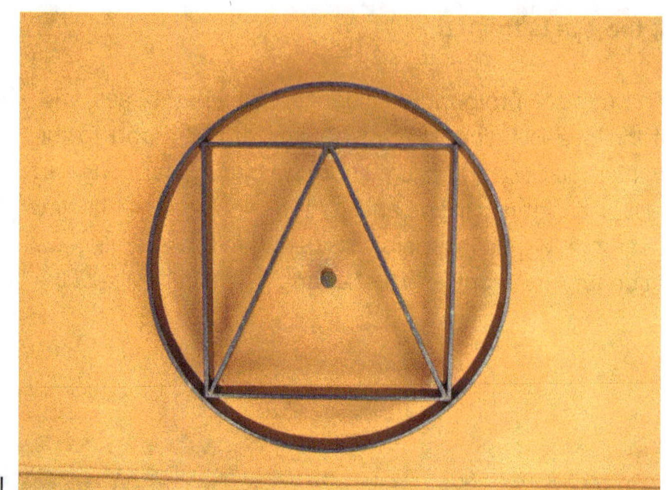

Ceramic mosaic by Kratu at Transition School

Making Life and Being beautiful

The preoccupation with universal beauty even in its aesthetic forms has an intense power for refining and subtilising the nature, and at its highest it is a great force for purification.

Sri Aurobindo

New beauty which wants to manifest

Perhaps in ten years there will be people who have found a new expression. A great progress would be necessary, an immense progress in the technique; the old technique seems barbarous. And now with the new scientific discoveries perhaps the technique of execution will change and one could find a new technique which would then express this new beauty which wants to manifest.

The Mother

Pyramid house

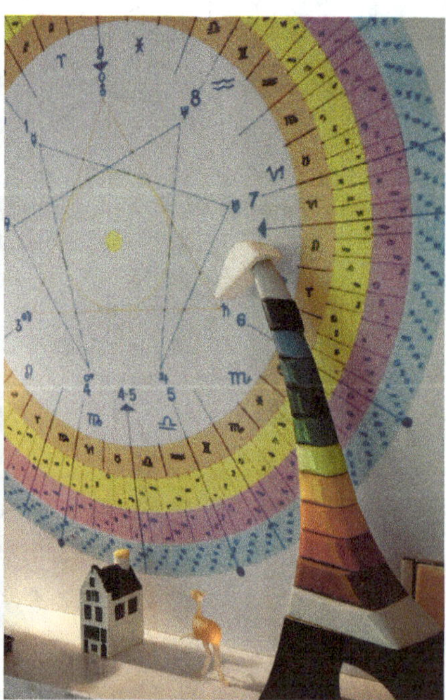

Marvellous possible universe

It seems beyond question to me that the universe in which we live is not one of the most successful, particularly in its outermost expression; but it is also beyond question

that we are part of it, and that consequently the only logical and wise thing for us to do is to set to work to perfect it, to extract the best from the worst and to make it into the most marvellous possible universe. For, I would add, not only is this transfiguration possible, but it is certain.

The perfect society

A complete and universal appreciation of beauty and the making entirely beautiful our whole life and being must surely be a necessary character of the perfect individual and the perfect society.

Sri Aurobindo

The pursuit of truth and beauty

The pursuit of truth and beauty is a sphere of activity in which we are permitted to remain children all our lives.

Albert Einstein

Residential house

Aluminium-clad house

At Auroville nothing belongs to anyone in particular. All is collective property. To be utilised with my blessings for the welfare of all.

The Mother

The sense of beauty is the powerful help

The work of purifying conduct through outward form and habitual and seemly regulation of expression, manner and action is the lowest of the many services which the artistic sense has done to humanity, and yet how wide is the field it covers and how important and indispensable have its workings been to the progress of civilisation! A still more important and indispensable activity of the sense of beauty is the powerful help it has given to the formation of morality.

Sri Aurobindo

Things of taste and beauty

Art galleries cannot be brought into every home, but, if all the appointments of our life and furniture of our homes are things of taste and beauty, it is inevitable that the habits, thoughts and feelings of the people should be raised, ennobled, harmonised, made more sweet and dignified.

Sri Aurobindo

The object of existence

A still more important and indispensable activity of the sense of beauty is the powerful help it has given to the formation of morality. We do not ordinarily recognise how largely our sense of virtue is a sense of the beautiful in conduct and our sense of sin a sense of ugliness and deformity in conduct. ...

The object of existence is not the practice of virtue for its own sake but *ānanda*, delight, and progress consists not in rejecting beauty and delight, but in rising from the lower to the higher, the less complete to the more complete beauty and to delight.

Sri Aurobindo

Residential house

There is a rhythm in everything

There is a rhythm in everything unheard by the physical ear and by that rhythm things exist.

Sri Aurobindo

Music, art and poetry are a perfect education for the soul

Between them music, art and poetry are a perfect education for the soul; they make and keep its movements purified, self-controlled, deep and harmonious. These, therefore, are agents which cannot profitably be neglected by humanity on its onward march or degraded to the mere satisfaction of sensuous pleasure which will disintegrate rather than build the character. They are, when properly used, great educating, edifying and civilising forces.

Sri Aurobindo

Care of material things

Not to take care of the material objects one uses is a sign of unconsciousness and ignorance.

One has no right to use any material object unless one takes care of it.

...we must take care of them, not because we are attached to them, but because they too manifest something of the Divine Consciousness.

The Mother

Respect for the objects one has

There is a kind of respect for the object one has, which must make one treat it with much consideration and try to preserve it as long as possible, not because one is attached to it and desires it, but because an object is something respectable which has sometimes cost a lot of effort and labour in the producing and so must as a result be considered with the respect due to the work and effort put into it.

The Mother

The Lord is everywhere, in everything

The Lord is everywhere, in everything, in what we throw away as in what we keep preciously, in what we trample on as in what we adore. We must learn to live with respect and never forget His constant and immutable Presence.

The Mother

Blue Clouds

Shakti, Force

Shakti, Force, pouring through the universe supports its boundless activities, the frail and tremulous life of the rose no less than the flaming motions of sun and star.

Sri Aurobindo

Quilts by Franz Fassbender

Henk van Putten

128

Beauty and delight, whatever form it takes, – for we may speak here of the two as one, – has an unaging youth, an eternal moment, an immortal presence.

Sri Aurobindo

Studio of Pierre le Grand

Art can express eternal truth

Art can express eternal truth, it is not limited to the expression of form and appearance. So wonderfully has God made the world that a man using a simple combination of lines, an unpretentious harmony of colours, can raise this apparently insignificant medium to suggest absolute and profound truths with a perfection which language labours with difficulty to reach. What Nature is, what God is, what man is can be triumphantly revealed in stone or on canvas.

Sri Aurobindo

To become more and more conscious

The discipline of art has at its centre the same principle as the discipline of Yoga. In both the aim is to become more and more conscious; in both you have to learn to see and feel something that is beyond the ordinary vision and feeling, to go within and bring out from there deeper things. Painters have to follow a discipline for the growth of the consciousness of their eyes, which in itself is almost a Yoga.

The Mother

Citadines

Studio of
Monique Patenaude

Art must serve as the revealer and teacher

True art means the expression of beauty in the material world. In a world wholly converted, that is to say, expressing integrally the divine reality, art must serve as the revealer and teacher of this divine beauty in life.

The Mother

Collages by Roger Anger

Next two pages: Sketches from Roger Anger's note book

l'oiseau en cage.

What is true art?

An artist should be capable of entering into com-
munion with the Divine and of receiving inspiration
about what form or forms ought to be used to express
the divine beauty in matter. And thus, if it does that,
art can be a means of realisation of beauty, and at the

"About Ram" by Anurupa Roy, play in Adishakti

same time a teacher of what beauty ought to be, that is art should be an element in the education of men's taste, of young and old, and it is the teaching of true beauty, that is, the essential beauty which expresses the divine truth. This is the *raison d'être of art.*

The Mother

Only this moment is life

Drink your tea slowly and reverently, as if it is the axis on which the world, the earth revolves – slowly, evenly, without rushing toward the future. Live the actual moment. Only this moment is life.

Thich Nhat Hanh

Kenji Matsumoto

Ikebana by Valeria Raso Matsumoto
and her students

LiGHT-FiSH

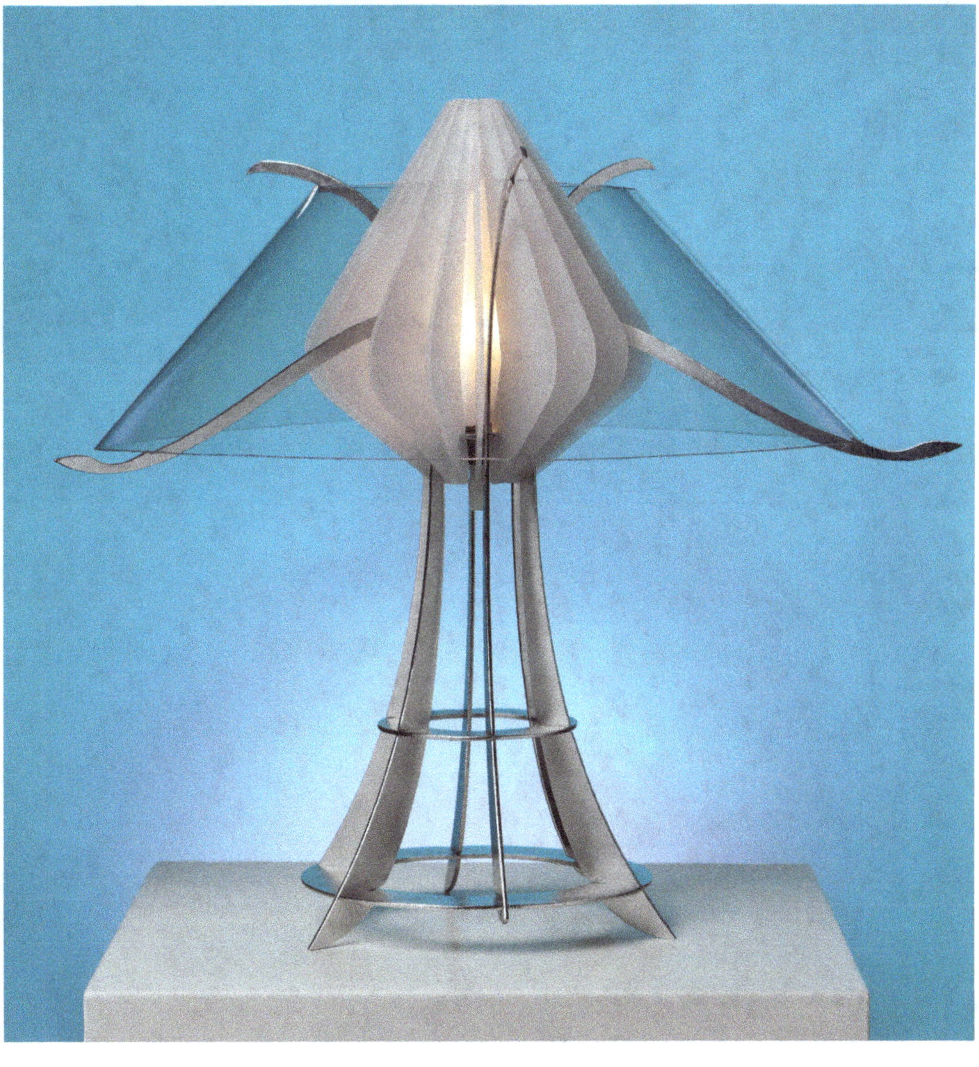

Svaram Musical Instruments and Research

Alternative energy systems

Auroville has the highest concentration of alternative and appropriate energy systems in India, including solar, wind and biogas generating systems. Of particular interest are the huge 15-metre diameter solar collector installed on the roof of the Solar Kitchen, designed to generate enough steam to cook over 1,000 meals a day, and the Matrimandir Solar Power Plant, the largest stand-alone system in India, comprising 484 photovoltaic modules

with total capacity of **36.3 KW**. Some **750** homes and / or
offices operate entirely or mostly on solar power.

15m diameter solar collector on the roof of the Solar Kitchen

Art for Art's sake

Art for Art's sake? But what, after all, is meant by this slogan and what is the real issue behind it? Is it meant, as I think it was when the slogan first came into use, that the technique, the artistry is all in all? The contention would then be that it does not matter what you write or paint or sculpt or what music you make or about what you make it so long as it is beautiful writing, competent painting, good sculpture, fine music. It is very evidently true in a certain sense, – in this sense that whatever is perfectly expressed or represented or interpreted under the conditions of a given art proves itself by that very fact to be legitimate material for the artist's labour.

But that free admission cannot be confined only to all objects, however common or deemed to be vulgar, – an apple, a kitchen pail, a donkey, a dish of carrots, – it can give a right of citizenship in the domain of art to a moral theme or thesis, a philosophic conclusion, a social experiment; even the Five Years' Plan or the proceedings of a District Board or the success of a drainage scheme, an electric factory or a big hotel can be brought, after the most modern or the still more robustious Bolshevik mode, into the artist's province. For, technique being all, the sole question would be whether he as poet, novelist, dramatist, painter or sculptor has been able to triumph over the difficulties and bring out creatively the possibilities of his subject. There is no logical basis here for accepting an apple and rejecting the Apple-Cart.

But still you may say that at least the object of the artist must be art only, – even if he treats ethical, social or political questions, he must not make it his main object to win with the enthusiasm of aesthetic creation a moral, social or political aim. But if in doing it he satisfies the conditions of his art, shows a perfect technique and in it beauty, power, perfection, why not? The moralist, preacher, philosopher, social or political enthusiast is often doubled with an artist – as shining proofs and examples there are Plato and Shelley, to go no farther. Only, you can say of him on the basis of this theory that as a work of art his creation should be judged by its success of craftsmanship and not by its contents; it is not made greater by the value of his ethical ideas, his enthusiasms or his metaphysical seekings.

But here, again, what after all is Beauty?

But then, the theory itself is true only up to a certain point. For technique is a means of expression; one does not write merely to use beautiful words or paint for the sole sake of line and colour; there is something that one is trying through these means to express or to discover. What is that something? The first answer would be – it is the creation, it is the discovery of Beauty.

Art is for that alone and can be judged only by its revelation or discovery of Beauty. Whatever is capable of being manifested as Beauty is the material of the artist. But there is not only physical beauty in the world – there is moral, intellectual, spiritual beauty also. Still, one might say that "Art for Art's sake" means that only what is aesthetically beautiful must be expressed and all that contradicts the aesthetic sense of beauty must be avoided.

Art has nothing to do with life in itself, things in themselves, Good, Truth or the Divine for their own sake, but only in so far as they appeal to some aesthetic sense of beauty, – and that would seem to be a sound basis for excluding the Five Years' Plan, a moral sermon or a philosophical treatise.

But here, again, what after all is Beauty? How much is it in the thing itself and how much in the consciousness that perceives it? Is not the eye of the artist constantly catching some element of aesthetic value in the plain, the ugly, the sordid, the repellent and triumphantly conveying it through his material, – through the word, through line and colour, through the sculptured shape?

Art is discovery and revelation of Beauty

There is a certain state of Yogic consciousness in which all things become beautiful to the eye of the seer, simply because they spiritually are, – because they are a rendering in line and form of the quality and force of existence, of the consciousness, of the Ananda that rules the worlds, – of the hidden Divine. What a thing is to the exterior sense may not be, often is not beautiful for the ordinary aesthetic vision, but the Yogin sees in it the something more which the external eye does not see, he sees the soul behind, the self and spirit, he sees too lines, hues, harmonies and expressive dispositions which are not to the first surface sight visible or seizable.

It may be said that he brings into the object something that is in himself, transmutes it by adding out of his own being to it – as the artist too does something of the same kind but in another way. It is not quite that, however; what the Yogin sees, what the artist sees, is there, his is a transmuting vision because it is a revealing vision; he discovers behind what the object appears to be, the something More that it is. And so from this point of view of a realised supreme harmony all is or can be subject-matter for the artist, because in all he can discover and reveal the Beauty that is everywhere. Again, we land ourselves in a devastating catholicity; for here too one cannot pull up short at any given line.

It may be a hard saying that one must or may discover and reveal beauty in a pig or its poke or in a parish pump or an advertisement of somebody's pills, and yet something like that seems to be what modern Art and Literature are trying with vigour and conscientious

labour to do. By extension one ought to be able to extract beauty equally well out of morality or social reform or a political caucus or allow at least that all these things can, if he wills, become legitimate subjects for the artist. Here, too, one cannot say that it is on condition he thinks of beauty only and does not make moralising or social reform or a political idea his main object. For if with that idea foremost in his mind he still produces a great work of art, discovering Beauty as he moves to his aim, proving himself in spite of his unaesthetic preoccupations a great artist, it is all we can justly ask from him, whatever his starting-point, to be a creator of Beauty. Art is discovery and revelation of Beauty, and we can say nothing more by way of prohibitive or limiting rule.

Some things are more divine than others

But there is one thing more that can be said, and that makes a big difference. In the Yogin's vision of universal beauty, all becomes beautiful, but all is not reduced to a single level. There are gradations, there is a hierarchy in this All-Beauty and we see that it depends on the ascending power *(Vibhūti)* of Consciousness and Ananda that expresses itself in the object.

All is the Divine, but some things are more divine than others. In the artist's vision too there can be gradations, a hierarchy of values. Shakespeare can get dramatic and therefore aesthetic values out of Dogberry and Malvolio and he is as thorough a creative artist in his treatment of them as in his handling of Macbeth or Lear. But if we had only Dogberry or Malvolio to testify to Shakespeare's genius, no Macbeth, no Lear, would he be so great a dramatic artist and creator as he now is?

It is in the varying possibilities of one subject or another that there lies an immense difference. Apelles' grapes deceived the birds that came to peck at them, but there was more aesthetic content in the Zeus of Pheidias, a greater content of Consciousness and therefore of Ananda to express and with it to fill in and intensify the essential principle of Beauty, even though the essence of beauty may be realised perhaps with equal aesthetic perfection by either artist and in either theme.

Art it is a self-expression of Consciousness

And that is because just as technique is not all, so even Beauty is not all in Art. Art is not only technique or form of Beauty, not only the discovery or the expression of Beauty – it is a self-expression of Consciousness under the conditions of aesthetic vision and a perfect execution. Or, to put it otherwise, there are not only aesthetic values, but life-values, mind-values, soul-values that enter into Art.

The artist puts out into form not only the powers of his own consciousness, but the powers of the Consciousness that has made the worlds and their objects. And if that Consciousness according to the Vedantic view is fundamentally equal everywhere, it is still in manifestation not an equal power in all things. There is more of the Divine expression in the *Vibhūti* than in the common man, *prākrito* janah; in some forms of life there are less potentialities for the self-expression of the Spirit than in others. And there are also gradations of consciousness which make a difference, if not in the aesthetic value or greatness of a work of art, yet in its contents-value.

Homer makes beauty out of man's outward life and action and stops there. Shakespeare rises one step further and reveals to us a life-soul and life-forces and life-values to which Homer had no access. In Valmiki and Vyas there is the constant presence of great Idea-Forces and Ideals supporting life and its movements which were beyond the scope of Homer and Shakespeare. And beyond the Ideals and Idea-Forces even there are other presences, more inner or inmost realities, a soul behind things and beings, the spirit and its powers, which could be the subject-matter of an art still more rich and deep and abundant in its interest than any of these could be.

A poet finding these and giving them a voice with a genius equal to that of the poets of the past might not be greater than they in a purely aesthetic valuation, but his art's contents-value, its consciousness-values could be deeper and higher and much fuller than in any achievement before him. There is something here that goes beyond any consideration of Art for Art's sake or Art for Beauty's sake; for while these stress usefully sometimes the indispensable first elements of artistic creation, they would limit too much the creation itself if they stood for the exclusion of the something More that compels Art to change always in its constant seeking for more and that must be expressed of the concealed or the revealed Divine, of the individual and the universal or the transcendent Spirit.

If we take these three elements as making the whole of Art, perfection of expressive form, discovery of beauty, revelation of the soul and essence of things and the powers of creative consciousness and Ananda of which they are the vehicles, then we shall get perhaps a solution which includes the two sides of the controversy and reconciles their difference.

Art for Art's sake certainly; Art as a perfect form and discovery of Beauty; but also Art for the soul's sake, the spirit's sake and the expression of all that the soul, the spirit wants to seize through the medium of beauty. In that self-expression there are grades and hierarchies, widenings and steps that lead to the summits. And not only to enlarge Art towards the widest wideness but to ascend with it to the heights that climb towards the Highest is and must be part both of our aesthetic and our spiritual endeavour.

April 17, 1933

Creation by the word

I do not know what to say on the subject you propose to me—my appreciation of music is bodiless and inexpressible, while about poetry I can write at ease with an expert knowledge. But is it necessary to fix a scale of greatness where each has its own greatnesses and can touch in its own way the extremes of aesthetic Ananda ? Music, no doubt, goes nearest to the infinite and to the essence of things because it relies wholly on the ethereal vehicle, *Śabda* [sound], (architecture by the by can do something of the same kind at the other extreme even in its imprisonment in mass); but painting and sculpture have their revenge by liberating visible form into ecstasy, while poetry though it cannot do with sound what music does, yet can instead make a harmony of sound revelation, creation by the word, suggestion of form and colour that gives it in a very subtle kind the combined power of all the arts. Who shall decide between such claims or be a judge between these gods?

Letter from Sri Aurobindo to Dilip Kumar Roy, April 26, 1933

Contact details

General information on Auroville:
info@auroville.org.in

Public relations:
outreachmedia@auroville.org.in

Auroville International website:
www.auroville-international.org

Auroville website:
www.auroville.org

Adil Writer
adil@auroville.org.in
www.adilwriter.com

Adishakti
adishakti@satyam.net.in
www.adishaktitheatrearts.com

Ange Peter
ange@auroville.org.in
www.forest-pottery.com

Dustudio
dharmesh@auroville.org.in

Franz Fassbender
franz@auroville.org.in

Henk van Putten
agnusandhenk@auroville.org.in
www.henkvanputten.com

Kenji Matsumoto
kenval@auroville.org.in
www.japaneseartfurniture.com

Light-Fish
Samvit Blass, sblass@light-fish.com
www. light-fish.com

Monique Patenaude
patenaude@auroville.org.in

Nele Martens
nele@auroville.org.in
www.nelemartens.net

Pierre le Grand
anu@auroville.org.in

Svaram Musical Instruments and Research
svaram@auroville.org.in
www.svaram.org

Shama Dalvi Architects
www.shamadalvi.com
info@shamadalvi.com

Valeria Raso Matsumoto
valeriaraso@hotmail.com
www.japaneseartfurniture.com

Acknowledgements

Photographs:

Photos: John Mandeen

Other photos:
Dominique Darr, pp. 6,7,8,9,10 (Top),11
Venkatesh, p.10 (bottom)
Giorgio Molinari, pp. 61,62,63,64,65, 100, 101
Franz Fassbender, pp.124, 125
Sven Ulsa, pp.142, 143
Ireno Guerci, pp.123, 148 (centre), 120
(bottom right), 119 (bottom two)
Mira Studio, p.149

We also thank Auroville Archives for making it
possible to use photos of Auroville's early years.

Designed and produced by:

PRISMA, Aurelec-Prayogashala,
Auroville 605101, Tamil Nadu, INDIA
prisma@auroville.org.in
Tel: +91-413-2622296
Fax: +91-413-2622185

Concept & Layout: Franz Fassbender
D.T.P. work: S. Janarthanan

© PRISMA
First edition: 2011
Second edition: 2015

Printed at:
Sudarsan Graphics, Chennai, INDIA

Text:

p. 6; Words of the Mother, 31 May 1969
p. 19; CWM 7:58
p. 20; CWM:124
p. 21; CWM 7:190
p. 23; CWM 3:109
p. 24; The National Value of Art, II
p. 26; The National Value of Art, III
p. 28; CWM 12:133
p. 29; The National Value of Art, VI
p. 31; CWM 12:129
p. 34; CWM 3:110
p. 38; The National Value of Art, V
p. 41; Sri Aurobindo's Action, September 2010
p. 44; Foundation of Indian Culture, Indian Art, II
p. 47; The National Value of Art, IV
p. 50; SABCL 20:495
p. 52; CWM 7:190
p. 55; The Mother's letter to Maurice Magre,
           Mother India, May 2011,
p. 56; SABCL 15:128
p. 60; Words of the Mother, 14 May 1970
p. 64; The National Value of Art, II
p. 66; The National Value of Art, IV
p. 68; The National Value of Art, III
p. 77; SABCL 23:1083
p. 78; The National Value of Art, IV
p. 80; CWM 17:87-88
p. 86; CWM 7:50
p. 88; CWM 16:256
p. 92; The National Value of Art, II
p. 94; Mahakalakshmi
p. 106; CWMCE, Questions and Answers
            28.7.1929
p. 108; The National Value of Art, V
p. 115; CWM 3:108
p. 125; The National Value of Art, V
p. 127; SABCL 9:235-236
p. 132; The National Value of Art, V
p. 134; CWM 3, 28.7.1929
p. 136; The National Value of Art, V
p. 162-146; Sri Aurobindo to Dilip, Volume 1,
            1929-1933, Hari Krishna Mandir
            Trust, Pune & Mira Aditi, Mysore,
            SABL Vol. 9, pp. 330-335